# Contents



Words in **bold** can be found in the glossary on page 28

# What is a waterside home?

A waterside home is a home that lies next to a river, a lake, a **canal** or by the sea. Some waterside homes are built over the water, and some **float** on the water itself.

▼ *These waterside homes are in the city of Sydney, Australia.*

Homes around the world

# Waterside homes

Nicola Barber

First published in Great Britain in 2006 by Wayland, an imprint of Hachette Children's Books



Hachette Children's Books
338 Euston Road, London NW1 3BH

Editor: Hayley Leach
Senior Design Manager: Rosamund Saunders
Designer: Elaine Wilkinson
Geography consultant: Ruth Jenkins

Printed and bound in China

British Library Cataloguing in Publication Data
Barber, Nicola
Waterside home. - (Homes around the world)
1.Dwellings - Juvenile literature
I.Title
643.1'09146

ISBN-10: 0750248742
ISBN-13: 978-0-7502-4874-7

Cover photograph: Brightly painted houses line a canal on the island of Burano in Venice, Italy.

Photo credits: Fraser Hall/Robert Harding World Imagery/Getty Images 6; Guenter Rossenbach/zefa/ Corbis cover and 7; Gunter Grafenhain/A1 Pix Ltd 8; Paul A Souders/Corbis 9; Hugh Sitton Photography/Alamy 10 and 26; Robert Francis/ Robert Harding World Imagery/Getty Images 11; Holger Leue/Lonely Planet Images 2000 title page and 12; Vera Schimetzek/Alamy 13 and 27; Patrick Frilet/Rex Features 14; John Elk III/Lonely Planet Images 2000 15; Dennis M. Sabangan/ epa/Corbis 16; Jim West/Alamy 17; Roger Bamber/ Alamy 18; Collart Herve/Corbis Sygma 19; Craig Lovell/Alamy 20; John Maier Jr/Lonely Planet Images 2000 21; David Wall/Lonely Planet Images 2000 22; Jeremy Horner/Panos Pictures 23; Dermot Tatlow/Panos Pictures 24; Anders Blomqvist/Lonely Planet Images 2000 25.

In some places there are whole cities of waterside homes. The city of Venice in Italy is a waterside city. It is built on 118 small islands inside a **lagoon**. In Venice, people drive boats along the city's canals to get around the city.

▲ *Brightly painted houses line a canal on the island of Burano in Venice, Italy.*

## Waterside life

Venice has about 150 canals crossed by around 400 bridges.

# Old and new homes

In the past, people often built their homes near rivers. They used the water for cooking, drinking and washing. Homes were often built where people could cross easily from one side of a river to another. Sometimes a bridge was built to cross the river.

▼ *The town of Monschau in Germany lies on the Rur river. These houses are around 300 years old.*

In many towns and cities, there are big buildings called **warehouses** alongside rivers. The warehouses were once used for storing goods, such as food. Many warehouses have been **converted** into large **apartments** for people to live in.

*▲ These warehouses in Alesund, Norway, were once used to store fish. Today, they are people's homes.*

# Floating homes

The Uros people live high in the Andes Mountains of South America, on Lake Titicaca. They live on floating islands made out of **reeds**. The reeds grow in the lake. They build their homes out of mats made from the reeds.

▼ *This woman sits in front of her home on a floating island. The Uros people make boats out of reeds, too.*

Some people live in boats. This kind of boat is called a houseboat. People cook and eat, play and sleep, and even work on their boats. Many people who live on houseboats work as fishermen.

▲ *These houseboats are in Aberdeen* ***harbour*** *on Hong Kong Island.*

# Building a waterside home

People sometimes build their homes over the water. They push long wooden poles deep into the earth under the water to make **stilts**. In some places, people use a kind of plant called **rattan** to tie all the different bits of wood together.

*In Kampong Ayer in Brunei, there are over 3,000 waterside homes on stilts. The houses are made from wood.*

In the Netherlands, there are floating houses that sit on **hollow** bottoms made from **concrete**. When it rains, the houses float up as the water rises. The houses slide up and down steel poles to stop them floating away.

## Waterside life

The floating houses on the River Maas can go up and down 5.5 metres on their steel poles.

▲ *This floating house lies on the River Maas in the Netherlands. The house has a roof made from metal.*

# Inside a waterside home

Houseboats are very popular in places such as Amsterdam in the Netherlands. Some houseboats are quite small inside, but others are big, with an upstairs and a downstairs. Old houseboats are often painted in bright colours inside and outside.

*This houseboat floats on the Canal du Centre in France. It is large and comfortable inside.*

In the town of Chau Doc in Vietnam, many people live in floating homes on the Bassac River. Some of them keep fish in nets in the water underneath their homes. They feed and catch the fish by opening **trap doors** in the floors of their houses.

▲ *Two boys feed the fish in the nets beneath their floating home.*

## Waterside life

There are about 1,000 fish farming families in Chau Doc.

# The weather

**Floods** can be a danger for people who have waterside homes. If there is a lot of rain, the water in rivers can rise above the river banks and cover the land. The water can fill homes. People often have to be rescued by boat, or by helicopter.

*This family in the Philippines is trapped on the roof of their home by floods. They are waiting to be rescued.*

Sometimes, storms hit towns and cities that are built by the sea. In 2005, there was a very strong storm called **Hurricane** Katrina. It hit the city of New Orleans in the United States. Almost all of the city was flooded after the hurricane.

▲ *A couple look inside their ruined home after the floods caused by Hurricane Katrina in New Orleans.*

# The environment

People may have to leave their seaside homes because of **erosion**. Erosion happens as the waves gradually wash away parts of the coastline. In places where the rocks are soft, the waves wash away the land more quickly than where the rocks are hard.

*These homes on the English coast once stood far from the **cliff** edge. Waves are washing the rocks of the cliff away.*

In some places, living by the water is not very **healthy**. In waterside **shanty towns**, it can be difficult for people to find clean water for drinking and cooking. But if they use dirty water, it can make them ill.

▲ *In this shanty town in Manaus, Brazil, the river water is dirty and full of rubbish.*

# School and play

In some parts of the world, children go to floating schools. In Cambodia there is a lake called Tonlé Sap. Most of the year the lake is small. Every year there is a time when lots of rain falls, and the lake floods. People have floating schools and homes on this lake.

▼ *Two boys return home from school through the waters of the Tonlé Sap in Cambodia.*

Children who live in waterside homes often love to play games together in the water. They learn to swim, sail boats, dive and to fish.

▲ *Children in Recife, Brazil, enjoy cooling off in the water near their homes.*

## Waterside life

When the Tonlé Sap floods it spreads to five times its normal size.

# Going to work

People who have waterside homes often go to work on the water. Fishermen catch fish in nets or with fishing lines. The town of Ganvié in Benin is a fishing town. It is built on stilts in Lake Nokwe. The fishermen use small boats called **canoes**.

▼ *Women paddle their canoes in Ganvié in Benin. Women sell the fish the men have caught at market.*

Many people like to take their holidays in beautiful waterside places. People who live on the coast or near lakes often work in shops, hotels or restaurants that are visited by **tourists**. In Thailand, tourists go to visit the floating market at Ratchaburi.

▲ *The floating market in Ratchaburi happens every day. People sell fresh fruit and vegetables from their boats.*

# Getting about

People who live near the water use boats to travel around. In places where there are no roads, going by boat is often the only way to get from one place to another. In the Amazon rainforest, **ferries** take supplies to far-away villages.

*This boat carries a doctor to a village on the Amazon River. It visits the village every two months.*

In some places, bridges join waterside **settlements**. Some bridges carry cars and other **vehicles**. Others carry trains.

▲ *This bridge joins Malmö in Sweden and Copenhagen in Denmark. It is called the Öresund Link.*

## Waterside life

The Öresund Link has two **decks**. Trains run on the lower deck, and there is a road on the upper deck.

# Where in the world?

Some of the places talked about in this book have been labelled here. ▼

## Look at these two pictures carefully.

- How are the homes different from each other?
- What is each home made of?
- Look at their walls, roofs, windows and doors.
- How are these homes different from where you live?
- How are they the same?

*Lake Titicaca, South America*

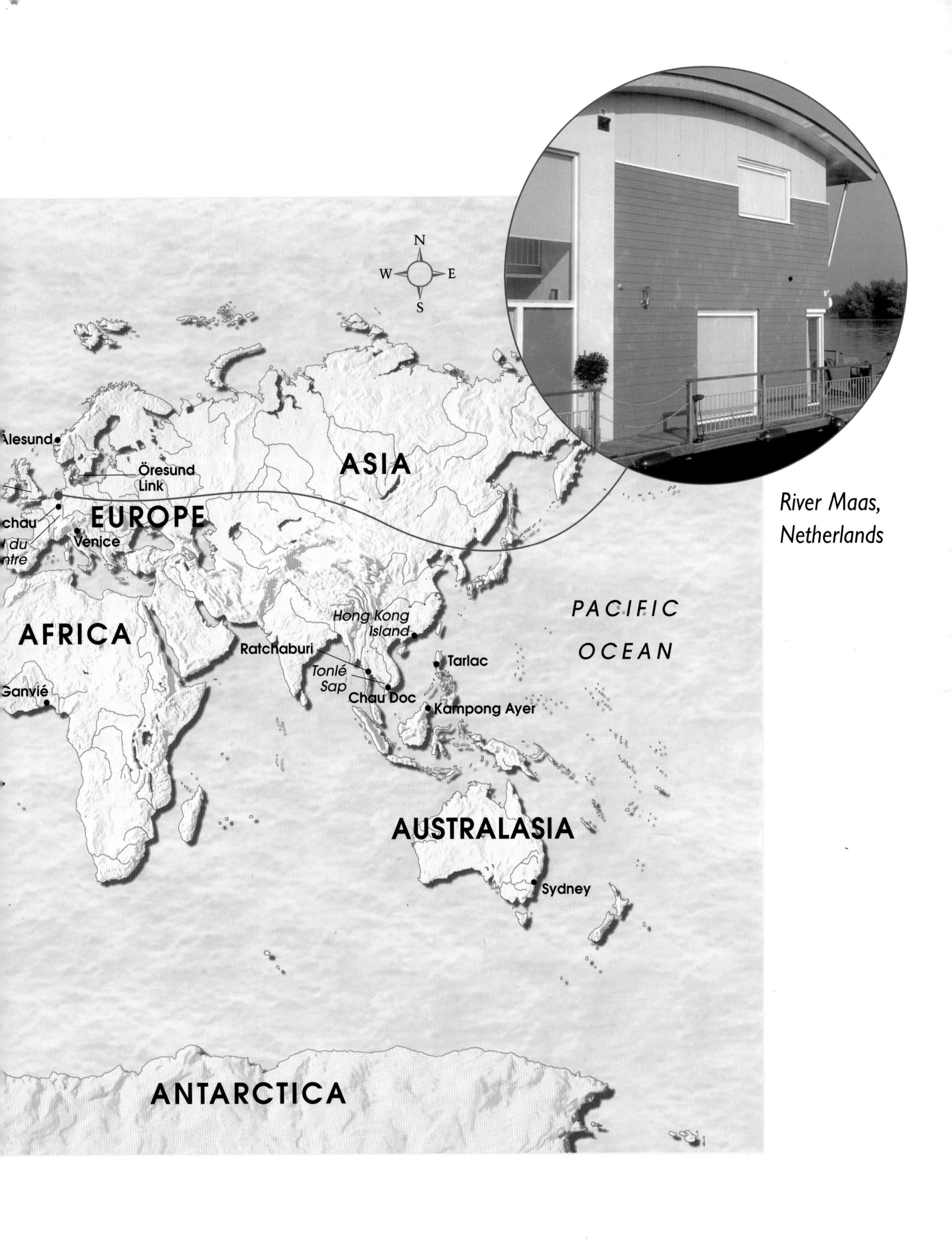


River Maas, Netherlands

# Glossary

| | |
|---|---|
| apartment | a set of rooms to live in, usually on one floor of a building |
| canal | a man-made channel of water |
| canoe | a small boat that is pushed along by paddles |
| cliff | a steep, high rock face |
| concrete | a mixture of cement, sand and water that gets harder as it dries |
| convert | to change into something else |
| deck | a floor often in a ship, or on a bridge |
| erosion | gradual wearing away, waves wear away soft rocks |
| ferry | a boat that carries people and vehicles from place to place |
| float | to be held up by water |
| flood | when water goes on to land that is normally dry |
| harbour | a safe place near land for boats to moor |
| healthy | when someone is fit and well |
| hollow | something that has an empty space inside |
| hurricane | a strong storm with high winds and lots of rain |
| lagoon | an area of sea water that is separated from the sea by a strip of land |
| rattan | a kind of climbing palm |
| reed | a kind of plant that grows in wet or marshy places |
| settlement | a place where people live |
| shanty towns | an area of roughly built homes |
| stilts | poles that are used to raise something off the ground |
| trap door | a small door in a floor or ceiling |
| tourist | a person who is on holiday |
| vehicle | any kind of transport with wheels, such as a car or a truck |
| warehouse | a large building used to store goods |

# Further information

## Books to read

*Geography First: Islands* Christopher Durbin, Wayland (2004)
*Geography First: Rivers* Nicola Edwards, Wayland (2004)
*Starters: Homes* Rosie McCormick, Wayland (2003)
*Around the World: Homes* Margaret Hall, Heinemann (2003)

## Websites

*http://www.worldlakes.org/index.asp*
To find out about lakes all around the world

*http://news.nationalgeographic.com/kids/*
National Geographic website for children

*http://www.bbc.co.uk/schools/riversandcoasts/rivers/people_river/index.shtml*
*http://www.bbc.co.uk/schools/riversandcoasts/coasts/people_coast/index.shtml*
Find out what it is like living near a river or on the coast

# Index

All the numbers in **bold** refer to photographs.